Cornerstones of Freedom

The Bill of Rights

R. Conrad Stein

CP CHILDRENS PRESS ®

CHICAGO

Congress OF THE United States

begun and held at the City of New-York, on
Wednesday the fourth of March, one thousand and seven hundred and eighty nine

THE Conventions of a number of the States, having at the time of their adopting the Constitution, expressed a desire, in order to prevent misconstruction or abuse of its powers, that further declaratory and restrictive clauses should be added: And as extending the ground of public confidence in the Government, will best ensure the beneficent ends of its institution

RESOLVED by the Senate and House of Representatives of the United States of America, in Congress assembled, two thirds of both Houses concurring, that the following Articles be proposed to the Legislatures of the several States, as amendments to the Constitution of the United States, all, or any of which Articles, when ratified by three fourths of the said Legislatures, to be valid to all intents and purposes, as part of the said Constitution; viz.

ARTICLES in addition to, and Amendment of the Constitution of the United States of America, proposed by Congress, and ratified by the Legislatures of the several States, pursuant to the fifth Article of the original Constitution.

Article the first... After the first enumeration required by the first Article of the Constitution, there shall be one Representative for every thirty thousand, until the number shall amount to one hundred, after which, the proportion shall be so regulated by Congress, that there shall be not less than one hundred Representatives, nor less than one Representative for every forty thousand persons, until the number of Representatives shall amount to two hundred, after which the proportion shall be so regulated by Congress, that there shall not be less than two hundred Representatives, nor more than one Representative for every fifty thousand persons.

Article the second... No law, varying the compensation for the services of the Senators and Representatives, shall take effect, until an election of Representatives shall have intervened.

Article the third... Congress shall make no law respecting an establishment of religion, or prohibiting the free exercise thereof; or abridging the freedom of speech, or of the press; or the right of the people peaceably to assemble, and to petition the Government for a redress of grievances.

Article the fourth... A well regulated militia, being necessary to the security of a free State, the right of the people to keep and bear arms, shall not be infringed.

Article the fifth... No Soldier shall, in time of peace be quartered in any house, without the consent of the owner, nor in time of war, but in a manner to be prescribed by law.

Article the sixth... The right of the people to be secure in their persons, houses, papers, and effects, against unreasonable searches and seizures, shall not be violated, and no Warrants shall issue, but upon probable cause, supported by oath or affirmation, and particularly describing the place to be searched, and the persons or things to be seized.

Article the seventh... No person shall be held to answer for a capital, or otherwise infamous crime, unless on a presentment or indictment of a grand jury, except in cases arising in the land or naval forces, or in the Militia, when in actual service in time of War or public danger; nor shall any person be subject for the same offence to be twice put in jeopardy of life or limb; nor shall be compelled in any criminal case to be a witness against himself, nor be deprived of life, liberty, or property, without due process of law; nor shall private property be taken for public use, without just compensation.

Article the eighth... In all criminal prosecutions, the accused shall enjoy the right to a speedy and public trial, by an impartial jury of the State and district wherein the crime shall have been committed, which district shall have been previously ascertained by law, and to be informed of the nature and cause of the accusation; to be confronted with the witnesses against him; to have compulsory process for obtaining witnesses in his favor, and to have the assistance of counsel for his defense.

Article the ninth... In suits at common law, where the value in controversy shall exceed twenty dollars, the right of trial by jury shall be preserved, and no fact tried by a jury, shall be otherwise re-examined in any court of the United States, than according to the rules of the common law.

Article the tenth... Excessive bail shall not be required, nor excessive fines imposed, nor cruel and unusual punishments inflicted.

Article the eleventh... The enumeration in the Constitution, of certain rights, shall not be construed to deny or disparage others retained by the people.

Article the twelfth... The powers not delegated to the United States by the Constitution, nor prohibited by it to the States, are reserved to the States respectively, or to the people.

ATTEST,

Frederick Augustus Muhlenberg, Speaker of the House of Representatives.
John Adams, Vice-President of the United States, and President of the Senate.

John Beckley, Clerk of the House of Representatives.
Sam. A. Otis, Secretary of the Senate.

Library of Congress Cataloging-in-Publication Data

Stein, R. Conrad.
  The Bill of Rights / by R. Conrad Stein.

    p. cm. — (Cornerstones of freedom)
  Summary: Discusses the first ten amendments to the
Constitution and the rights which they are intended to
protect.
  ISBN 0-516-04853-8
  1. United States—Constitutional law—Amendments—
1st-10th—Juvenile literature. [1. United States—
Constitutional law—Amendments—1st-10th. 2. Civil
rights.] I. Title. II. Series.
KF4750.S74   1992
342.73'085—dc20   91-41541
[347.30285]   CIP
                                                      AC

It was a ghastly crime, but to veteran officers on the Arizona police force, not an uncommon one. In 1966, an unemployed truck driver named Ernesto Miranda kidnapped and raped an eighteen-year-old girl. Under questioning, Miranda admitted to the Arizona police that he had committed the terrible act. In court, Miranda was sentenced to a prison term of twenty-to-thirty years.

After the sentencing, the Miranda case—tragic as it was for the victim—seemed to be closed. But Miranda's lawyers appealed the decision. The lawyers claimed that the police had failed to tell Miranda that he had the right to remain silent during questioning and that he also had a right to consult with a lawyer. These rights, the lawyers pointed out, were guaranteed to Miranda under the Bill of Rights of the American Constitution. The United States Supreme Court agreed, and in the case *Miranda v. Arizona*, overturned the conviction. Miranda went free. Ever since the Miranda ruling, police officers

Ever since the case of Ernesto Miranda (left), police have been required to read criminal suspects the "Miranda Warning" (right), which explains certain rights guaranteed accused persons under the Bill of Rights.

CUSTODIAL INTERROGATION (MIRANDA) WARNING

After each part of the following warning, the officer must determine whether the suspect understands what he is being told:

1. You have a right to remain silent. You do not have to talk to me unless you want to do so.

2. If you do want to talk to me, I must advise you that whatever you say can and will be used as evidence against you in court.

3. You have a right to consult with a lawyer and to have a lawyer present with you while you are being questioned.

4. If you want a lawyer but are unable to pay for one, a lawyer will be appointed to represent you free of any cost to you.

5. Knowing these rights, do you want to talk to me without having a lawyer present? You may stop talking to me at any time and you may also demand a lawyer at any time.

have been required to read a person his or her rights immediately after making an arrest.

In the instance of Ernesto Miranda, a confessed criminal escaped punishment because of provisions in the Bill of Rights. The Bill of Rights was not written to aid lawbreakers, however. Instead, it was intended to protect individuals from the awesome powers of government. The need for such protection was understood more than two hundred years ago by the men who wrote the United States Constitution.

When the bloody Revolutionary War ended in 1783, Americans began putting their shattered country together. Their most important task was to form a national government to unite the thirteen newly formed states. During the sweltering summer of 1787, twelve of the states sent delegates to a meeting in Philadelphia. This meeting came to be called the Constitutional Convention. In Philadelphia, the delegates argued, compromised, and laboriously wrote the United States Constitution. James Madison, who is often called the Father of the Constitution, told the delegates that the work they were doing "would decide forever the fate of republican government."

James Madison

George Washington speaking at the Constitutional Convention

The United States Constitution

As written, the Constitution was an amazing document. It provided rules for running the American government that have endured for more than two hundred years. Still, not all the delegates at the Constitutional Convention were satisfied. The Constitution failed to guarantee the American people individual rights—precious liberties such as freedom of speech, freedom of

Elbridge Gerry (left), George Mason (center), and Edmund Randolph (right) refused to sign the U.S. Constitution largely because it failed to include a declaration of individual rights.

the press, and freedom of religion. Three of the delegates—Elbridge Gerry, George Mason, and Edmund Randolph—refused to sign the Constitution largely because it contained no specific guarantee of individual liberties. George Mason, a scholarly planter from Virginia, was particularly insistent on writing a bill of rights. Mason argued that such a declaration "would give great quiet to the people."

Even without a declaration of human rights, the Constitution was eventually approved by the states, and it went into effect in June 1788. But many Americans continued to demand that protection of human rights be spelled out in their Constitution. One of the most influential men of the time, Thomas Jefferson, wrote, "A bill of rights is what the people are entitled to . . . and what no just government should refuse." This intense desire to see human rights written into the law had deep roots in the historical tradition on which American government was based.

England, the mother country of the United States, was a wellspring for human-rights declarations. The concept of writing human rights into law began in England in 1215. That year, a group of noblemen, unhappy with the way the country was being governed, forced King John to sign the *Magna Carta* (Great Charter). Although the Magna Carta did little to help the common Englishman, it was an important first step toward limiting the power of the king and declaring that even the government must comply with written law.

The English people who settled in the American colonies brought with them the belief that citizens are entitled to certain rights that cannot be taken away by the government. The charters of each of the thirteen colonies included a declaration of human rights. The colonists' passion for human rights is clearly seen in the famous words of the Declaration of Independence: "We hold these truths to be self-evident, that all men are created equal, that they are endowed by their Creator with certain unalienable rights, that among these are Life, Liberty, and the pursuit of Happiness."

The Magna Carta (right), signed by King John of England in 1215, laid the basis for the concept of writing human rights into law.

The United States Constitution was barely a year old when government leaders, headed by James Madison, moved to add a declaration of human rights to the document. Madison and other members of the first Congress proposed twelve amendments (changes) to the Constitution. Ten of these amendments—which came to be known as the Bill of Rights—were approved by the states and became a permanent

In 1941, President Franklin D. Roosevelt proclaimed December 15 as Bill of Rights Day.

addition to the Constitution on December 15, 1791. Today, December 15 is celebrated in the United States as Bill of Rights Day. Bill of Rights Day was first proclaimed in 1941 by President Franklin D. Roosevelt.

Briefly, the Bill of Rights can be summed up as follows. The First Amendment guarantees the people freedom of speech, freedom of religious expression, and the freedom to assemble peacefully. The Second Amendment protects the right of citizens to bear arms. The Third and Fourth amendments assure the right to privacy by stating, among other things, that a home cannot be entered by police without the owner's permission except under circumstances prescribed by law. The Fifth, Sixth, Seventh, and Eighth amendments protect people accused of crimes by guaranteeing certain rights, including trial by jury. Amendments nine and ten forbid Congress from passing any law that would circumvent any of the first eight amendments.

At first, the Bill of Rights applied only to the federal government, not to the states. Americans of the 1790s looked upon the new federal government with fear. They believed that the actions of the state governments could be easily controlled, whereas the new national government loomed as a possible villain needing restrictions. Also, all the state constitutions already had declarations guaranteeing individual rights. In an 1833 case involving Maryland, the Supreme Court confirmed that the Bill of Rights put limits only on the federal government. Later, however, the court reversed the 1833 ruling, and today, provisions in the Bill of Rights are also applied to the states.

In the 1790s, the liberties guaranteed by the Bill of Rights did not extend to everyone; the nation's black slaves were a notable exception.

The Bill of Rights allows Americans to criticize the government publicly on any issue, including civil rights (above), economic policies (right), and the rights of disabled people (far right).

Slaves were considered property, not citizens. It took a bloody civil war in the 1860s and then a hundred more years of struggle before African Americans enjoyed the full freedoms offered by the Bill of Rights.

Today, most Americans think of the rights spelled out in the Bill of Rights as fundamental liberties. Certainly no reasonable American would want to see the first ten amendments rescinded. The Bill of Rights allows people to disagree with their government. The right to disagree is unquestioned in American society.

Nevertheless, all freedoms have limitations. No
one has the right to use their freedoms to justify
actions that might harm others. Americans
cherish the Bill of Rights, but they also realize
that the liberties it spells out must be regulated
in the face of real-life situations.

Freedom of speech, which is guaranteed by the
First Amendment, often forces society to make a
crucial choice between peace and chaos; between
preserving the rights of an individual and
safeguarding the rights of those around him.
Should white-hooded members of the Ku Klux

Flag burning, a highly controversial act of protest, is protected under the First Amendment's guarantee of freedom of speech.

Klan be allowed to parade through a black neighborhood shouting insults at African Americans? Can a Nazi group openly threaten to wage war on Jews? Supreme Court justice Oliver Wendell Holmes, Jr., once said, "The most stringent protection of free speech would not protect a man in falsely shouting 'Fire!' in a theater and causing a panic. [The] question in every case is whether the words used are used in such circumstances and are of such a nature as to create a clear and present danger that they will bring about the substantive evils that Congress has a right to prevent." Thus, a judge may forbid a person to speak, or a movie to be shown, or a book to be published, if the judge believes such expression will endanger the health, welfare, or safety of others. The government may also limit freedom of speech in cases where a person's form of expression urges people to riot, calls for the violent overthrow of the government, or threatens national security. Moreover, the First Amendment does not protect a person who tells lies that might damage a person's reputation. The process of limiting free expression is complicated, however, and usually settled in court.

Oliver Wendell Holmes, Jr.

A free-speech argument captured the nation's headlines in 1971, during the bitter era of the Vietnam War. Several newspapers had obtained copies of the Pentagon Papers, a "top-secret" government report detailing American involvement in southeast Asia. The report revealed many American dealings in the region that had been kept secret from the public. The *New York Times* wanted to publish the report, but a judge forbade the paper from doing so on the grounds that it might endanger national security. The Supreme Court overruled the judge, and allowed the *New York Times* to publish the Pentagon Papers. The court held that in this instance, freedom of speech was more important than national security.

Charles Evans Hughes

As in the case of the Pentagon Papers, the most important challenges to the Bill of Rights become court cases presented to the United States Supreme Court. The nine-member Supreme Court is the highest court in the land. Historically, it has the task of interpreting the United States Constitution. Charles Evans Hughes, who served on the Supreme Court in the 1930s, once said, "We are under a constitution, but the constitution is what judges say it is." A brief amendment-by-amendment look at the Supreme Court's interpretation of the Bill of Rights shows how the justices weigh words against circumstances on a delicate balancing scale.

Some of the most passionate arguments ever heard in the Supreme Court stem from the First

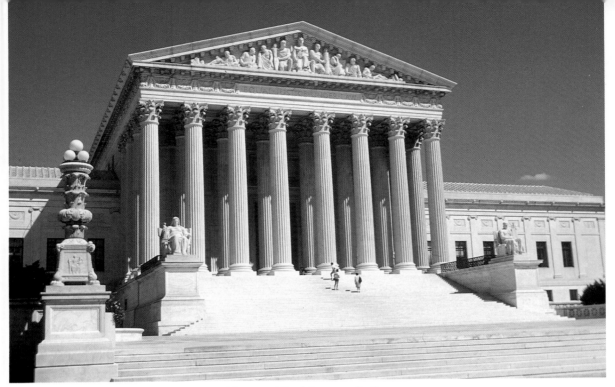

The Supreme Court Building in Washington, D.C.

Amendment and the issue of religion. The
opening words of the First Amendment are
"Congress shall make no law respecting an
establishment of religion . . ." This phrase means
that the government cannot set up a church and
force people to worship there. State-sponsored
churches were once common in European
countries. Never in its history has Congress
attempted to establish a government-supported
church. But what about prayer sessions held in
public schools? A generation ago, students at
most public schools were required to begin their
day by bowing their heads and saying a prayer.
Then, in 1962, a group of parents challenged
school prayer, claiming it amounted to the

"establishment of religion" and therefore was in violation of the First Amendment. The Supreme Court agreed, and today, organized prayer in public school is forbidden.

The First Amendment also guarantees Americans the freedom to worship as they choose. Again, what seems on the surface to be a simple and basic liberty can lead to complicated legal cases. What happens when freedom of worship conflicts with the duties of citizens? Can a Quaker, who has sworn never to fight or kill, refuse induction into the army during time of war? Can parents refuse medical treatment for their sick child on the grounds that their religion

The First Amendment guarantees Americans the freedom to worship as they choose.

In the 1960s, some young people burned their draft cards to symbolize their refusal to fight in the Vietnam War.

forbids such treatment? The questions involving religious freedom and the First Amendment are endless.

Over the years, the Supreme Court has struggled to resolve the problems arising from the freedom-of-religion aspects of the First Amendment. A rather common problem involves individuals who refuse to serve in the military on religious grounds. As early as World War I, Congress exempted members of certain religious sects from the draft law. Those people who claimed that their religion forbade them from entering the army were called conscientious objectors. Then, in 1957, a young man named Donald Seeger refused induction into the army on religious grounds even though he belonged to no specific religious group. The Supreme Court agreed that Seeger should be classified as a conscientious objector, ruling that church membership is not necessary to establish religious objections to serving in the military.

The issue of freedom of expression, which is guaranteed by the First Amendment, has been tested in thousands of cases, some involving the conduct of students in their classrooms. In 1965, thirteen-year-old Mary Beth Tinker and two other students in Des Moines, Iowa, wore black arm bands to school to protest the war in Vietnam.

Mary Beth Tinker and her mother

The school suspended them for violating the dress code. Mary Beth's father, a minister, sued the school system. The case reached the Supreme Court, which ruled in favor of the students, saying that wearing arm bands was a legitimate form of expression, and therefore protected by the First Amendment. In a 1988 case, a group of high-school students sued their school because the principal refused to publish a controversial story in the school newspaper. This time, the Supreme Court backed the principal, claiming that he, as the publisher of the paper, had the right to choose or reject any story he wished.

The Second and Third amendments rarely cause controversy today. The Second Amendment guarantees American citizens the right to bear arms. This amendment was included so that the federal government would not be able to disarm a state militia. At the time the Bill of Rights was written, no one could have dreamed of a time when hardened criminals carrying handguns would terrorize whole city neighborhoods. However, the Second Amendment prohibited only the *federal* government's ability to limit the right to carry a weapon. Individual states could still regulate the bearing of arms. Today, every state has some sort of gun-control law.

The Third Amendment states that the government cannot move soldiers into a private house without the permission of the owner. This

The Fourth Amendment protects citizens from being searched for no apparent reason, but police may search a person if there is cause to believe that he or she is concealing something illegal.

"quartering of troops" was once practiced in Europe, but it has never been a major problem in the United States.

It seems that every movie involving tough cops includes a scene where several police officers break down a door, rush inside a house, guns in hand, and shout, "Freeze, this is the police!" In most circumstances, however, police must have a search warrant signed by a judge in order to enter one's house. This is because the Fourth Amendment prohibits "unreasonable searches and seizures." The amendment also protects people from being stopped on the street and searched by police for no apparent reason.

However, the law is applied differently for people on the street than for searches of a home. The Supreme Court has ruled that police may search a person outside his home if they have "probable cause" to believe that the person is concealing something illegal. Also, in a 1972 case, the Supreme Court ruled that while making a lawful arrest, the police may search people, cars, and the area under their immediate control.

Professional criminals often use the Fourth Amendment to their advantage, and this causes great public outcry. Drug dealers, for example, know how to twist the intent of the words "unreasonable searches and seizures" to protect their drug supplies from police. Still, the public demands that the government do something to stop the spread of drugs. Judges respond by giving police greater authority to enter houses, tap telephone lines, and seize contraband. The increasing drug trafficking of the 1980s and 1990s not only made the streets dangerous, it also helped to erode the liberties guaranteed by the Fourth Amendment.

"I refuse to answer that question on the grounds that my answer may tend to incriminate me." These words have been droned out thousands of times in courtrooms and before Senate hearing committees. The people who make this statement are invoking their Fifth Amendment right against self-incrimination. This right is closely related to the basic principle of our criminal justice system—that a person is innocent until proven guilty. In our system, it is the burden of the court to prove that the accused person is guilty, and the accused is under no obligation to assist in this proof. Without the protection of the Fifth Amendment, prosecutors could question a person accused of a crime in such a way that the person might admit guilt without intending to do so, thus incriminating himself. The idea of protection against self-incrimination began ages ago in England, when people began opposing the government's use of torture as a way to extract evidence from an accused person.

William O. Douglas

In defense of self-incrimination restrictions, the famous Supreme Court justice William O. Douglas once wrote, "The Fifth Amendment was written in part to prevent any congress, any court, and any prosecutor from prying open the lips of an accused to make incriminating statements against his will." But although the Supreme Court has always protected Fifth-Amendment rights, prosecutors have been known to use the self-incrimination clause to their advantage.

During the great "Red Scare" of the 1950s, Wisconsin senator Joseph McCarthy grabbed national headlines by accusing government leaders and high-profile public figures of being

Actor Robert Taylor prepares to testify in front of a hearing led by Joseph McCarthy during the "Red Scare" of the 1950s.

Communists. At Senate hearings, McCarthy asked trick questions that forced witnesses to invoke their Fifth-Amendment rights and refuse to answer. Many Americans watching the hearings on television were led to believe that "taking the fifth" was the same as an admission of guilt. Despite his wild charges and vigorous prosecuting, McCarthy was unable to uncover even a single "card-carrying Communist" in any government department. Today, the McCarthy hearings are remembered as a "witch-hunt" that violated the rights of countless Americans.

Other clauses in the Fifth Amendment protect personal property and a citizen's rights in court.

The amendment provides that people arrested for serious crimes face a grand jury (a preliminary jury) shortly after their arrest. Another clause in the Fifth Amendment protects a person from double jeopardy, meaning he or she cannot be tried twice for the same crime. The amendment's final clause states that private property cannot be "taken for public use, without compensation." This clause protects a home owner if, for example, the government deems it necessary to tear down a house in order to widen a road.

The Sixth and Seventh amendments regulate court practices. The Sixth Amendment promises the accused a "speedy and public trial" and "the assistance of counsel for his defense" (the use of a lawyer). Lawyers for Ernesto Miranda, the unemployed truck driver, won their case in part because the Arizona police had failed to inform Miranda that he had the right to speak to an attorney before he made a confession.

The Supreme Court broadened a defendant's right to have counsel in the famous 1963 case involving Clarence Gideon, a part-time tavern keeper. Gideon, who had a long record for burglary, was arrested after police charged him with breaking into a pool room in Panama City, Florida. Gideon could not afford to hire a lawyer to help him prepare a defense, and a court found him guilty of burglary. Although he was a high-school dropout, Gideon read many law books while in jail. He wrote to the Supreme Court and asked for a retrial, arguing that under the Sixth Amendment, the state of Florida should have provided him with a lawyer free of charge since he was penniless. The Supreme Court agreed, and granted Gideon a new trial. In a 1972 case, the Supreme Court expanded the Gideon rule. Today, anyone facing the possibility of a jail sentence is provided with a lawyer even if he or she cannot afford to pay for one.

The Eighth Amendment requires the courts to set a punishment that fits the crime. The amendment restricts judges from demanding excess bail and thereby holding an accused

Clarence Gideon

Public whipping, common in the 1700s, was the sort of "cruel and unusual punishment" the Eighth Amendment was meant to abolish.

person in jail for a longer period than necessary. The Eighth Amendment also forbids "cruel and unusual punishment." At the time the Bill of Rights was written, lawbreakers in other countries were commonly whipped, branded with hot irons, or subjected to other terrible penalties.

The Ninth and Tenth amendments do not grant specific rights to citizens. Instead, these two amendments require Congress to pass no laws limiting the freedoms granted by other amendments. Even though the Bill of Rights is usually considered to be made up of the first ten amendments, only amendments one through eight spell out specific liberties to individuals.

The United States is not the only nation to have a bill of rights written into its constitution. Canada has its Canadian Charter of Rights and Freedoms, which guarantees Canadian citizens freedom of religion and speech, and bans discrimination based on race or gender. The French bill of rights, called the Declaration of the Rights of Man and of the Citizens, was adopted in 1789 when revolution swept the land and a war cry echoed, "Liberty, Equality, Fraternity." Oldest of all declarations of individual liberties is the English Bill of Rights, adopted in 1689. The Americans named their first ten amendments the Bill of Rights after this earlier English document. In 1948, the United Nations issued its Universal Declaration of Human Rights. The United Nations decree stressed that all the world's citizens should be treated equally in the eyes of the law.

The freedoms granted Americans by the Bill of Rights are written in the most general terms. It is the task of the court system to interpret those fundamental liberties. Yet the opinion of judges is influenced by the will of the public. Therefore, the interpretion of the Bill of Rights changes with the public mood. A movie banned as pornographic one year may be accepted another year as an artistic expression protected by the First Amendment. Limits on free speech also vary from time to time. Still, the Bill of Rights remains a cornerstone of American freedom.

People demonstrating in favor of the Persian Gulf War in 1991

Controversy and bitter arguments will always be connected with the Bill of Rights. Freedom of speech, for example, often gives one person the liberty to state a view that another person finds repulsive. But the rights protected by the first ten amendments are so vital to American democracy that it is worth the cost of controversy. As Supreme Court justice Robert Jackson once wrote, "Freedom is not limited to things that do not matter much. That would be a mere shadow of freedom. The test of [freedom's] substance is the right to differ as to things that touch the heart of the existing order."

United States Bill of Rights

Amendment 1

Congress shall make no law respecting an establishment of religion, or prohibiting the free exercise thereof; or abridging the freedom of speech, or of the press; or the right of the people peaceably to assemble, and to petition the government for a redress of grievances.

Amendment 2

A well-regulated militia being necessary to the security of a free State, the right of the people to keep and bear arms shall not be infringed.

Amendment 3

No soldier shall, in time of peace, be quartered in any house without the consent of the owner; nor in time of war but in a manner to be prescribed by law.

Amendment 4

The right of the people to be secure in their persons, houses, papers and effects, against unreasonable searches and seizures, shall not be violated, and no warrants shall issue but upon probable cause, supported by oath or affirmation, and particularly describing the place to be searched, and the persons or things to be seized.

Amendment 5

No person shall be held to answer for a capital or otherwise infamous crime, unless on a presentment or indictment of a grand jury, except in cases arising in the land or naval forces, or in the militia, when in actual service in time of war or public danger; nor shall any person be subject for the same offense to be twice put in jeopardy of life or limb; nor shall be compelled in any criminal case to be a witness against himself, nor be deprived of life, liberty, or property, without due process of law; nor shall private property be taken for public use, without just compensation.

Amendment 6

In all criminal prosecutions the accused shall enjoy the right to a speedy and public trial, by an impartial jury of the State and district wherein the crime shall have been committed, which district shall have been previously ascertained by law, and to be informed of the nature and cause of the accusation; to be confronted with the witnesses against him; to have compulsory process for obtaining witnesses in his favor, and to have the assistance of counsel for his defense.

Amendment 7

In suits at common law, where the value in controversy shall exceed twenty dollars, the right of trial by jury shall be preserved, and no fact tried by a jury shall be otherwise reexamined in any court of the United States than according to the rules of the common law.

Amendment 8

Excessive bail shall not be required, nor excessive fines imposed, nor cruel and unusual punishments inflicted.

Amendment 9

The enumeration in the Constitution of certain rights shall not be construed to deny or disparage others retained by the people.

Amendment 10

The powers not delegated to the United States by the Constitution, nor prohibited by it to the States, are reserved to the States respectively, or to the people.

INDEX

PHOTO CREDITS

Cover, AP/Wide World; 1, © David M. Doody/Tom Stack & Associates; 2, National Archives; 4 (left), AP/Wide World: 4 (right), Courtesy of Villa Park Police Department; 5 (both photos), North Wind; 6, © Jon Feingersh/Tom Stack & Associates; 7 (left), Independence National Historical Park Collection; 7 (center), AP/Wide World; 7 (right), Virginia State Library and Archive: 9 (left), Historical Pictures Service, Chicago; 9 (right), The Bettmann Archive; 10, Historical Pictures Service, Chicago; 12, 13 (left), UPI/Bettmann; 13 (right), AP/Wide World; 14, H. Armstrong Roberts; 15, 16 (top), AP/Wide World; 16 (bottom), Historical Pictures Service, Chicago; 17, Photri; 18 (both photos), © Camerique/H. Armstrong Roberts; 19, AP/Wide World; 20, *The Des Moines Register;* 22, © L. O'Shaughnessy/H. Armstrong Roberts; 24, 25, Historical Pictures Service, Chicago; 26, © Camerique/H. Armstrong Roberts; 27, AP/Wide World; 28, Historical Pictures Service, Chicago; 30, © Brian Parker/Tom Stack & Associates

Picture Identifications:
Cover: People demonstrating in front of the U.S. Capitol for legislation to end discrimination against disabled people
Page 1: The original copies of the Declaration of Independence, the U.S. Constitution, and the Bill of Rights in the National Archives Building in Washington, D.C.
Page 2: The Bill of Rights

Project Editor: Shari Joffe
Designer: Karen Yops
Cornerstones of Freedom Logo: David Cunningham

ABOUT THE AUTHOR

R. Conrad Stein was born and raised in Chicago. He enlisted in the Marine Corps at the age of eighteen and served for three years. He then attended the University of Illinois, where he received a bachelor's degree in history. He later studied in Mexico, earning an advanced degree from the University of Guanajuato. Mr. Stein is the author of many books, articles, and short stories for young people.

Mr. Stein lives in Chicago with his wife and their daughter Janna.